GUITARBASE
GUIDE
LEFT-
SCALES
BY RIKKY ROOKSBY

Wise Publications
London/ New York/ Paris/ Sydney/
Copenhagen/ Berlin/ Madrid/ Tokyo

Exclusive Distributors:
Music Sales Limited
8/9 Frith Street, London W1D 3JB, England.
Music Sales Corporation
257 Park Avenue South, New York, NY10010, USA.
Music Sales Pty Limited
120 Rothschild Avenue, Rosebery, NSW 2018, Australia.

Order No. AM970684
ISBN 0-7119-8901-X
This book © Copyright 2002 by Wise Publications

Written and arranged by Rikky Rooksby
Music processed by Digital Music Art
Cover design by Mike Bell
Book design, layout and editing by Sorcha Armstrong
Printed in the United Kingdom.

Your Guarantee of Quality
As publishers, we strive to produce every book to the
highest commercial standards.
The music has been freshly engraved and the book has been
carefully designed to minimise awkward page turns and to
make playing from it a real pleasure.

Music Sales' complete catalogue describes thousands of titles and
is available in full colour sections by subject, direct from Music
Sales Limited. Please state your areas of interest and send a
cheque/postal order for £1.50 for postage to: Music Sales Limited,
Newmarket Road, Bury St. Edmunds, Suffolk IP33 3YB.

www.musicsales.com

INTRODUCTION

Maybe you're just beginning to learn guitar, or maybe you know some chords. Maybe you would like to play solos, or perhaps you can solo but you are looking for some new ideas. In each instance this book will help you increase your skills and knowledge of the guitar.

There are many books of scales available but the vast majority are aimed at right-handed players. This scale book is prepared specially for left-handers.

Scales are excellent for finger practice. Played regularly with a metronome these patterns can help you increase your speed. Speed up the metronome slowly as you adjust to a given rate of notes per beat.

In this book you will find all the most used and useful scales, in all keys. Each scale is shown as an easy-to-follow 'fretboard diagram' with hints and tips to help you get the most out of it.

Whether it's pop, rock, blues, or soul, you'll never be lost for notes ever again!

Rikky Rooksby

HOW TO READ
SCALE BOXES

If you know how to read chord boxes, scale boxes won't be too unfamiliar.

Reading the box

The vertical lines represent the **strings**. The line on the furthest right is the bottom E string or 6th (the thickest string on your guitar). The line on the farthest left is the top E or 1st string (the thinnest string). The horizontal lines represent the **frets**. The 'o' symbol is an open string which is played as part of the scale.

Root notes

When you practise scales the convention is to start on the root and end at the root – whether that's an octave, two octaves or even three octaves higher.

This does not apply when you are using a pattern in the middle of a solo. The **root** notes of the scale are shown in black with white numbers.

Grey notes

Notes shaded in grey also belong to the scale but are either above or below the two-octave root-to-root pattern. Beware: if you start any scale with grey notes the scale will probably not sound right. This is because your ear will tend to think the first note you play is the root, regardless of where the actual root is. Watch out for arrows that indicate a change of position.

We've included these 'grey' notes because you might want to use them in solos or patterns, even though they're outside the two-octave scale.

Finger Numbering

The fingers are numbered from the index finger: 1, 2, 3, and 4.

SCALE DIAGRAM

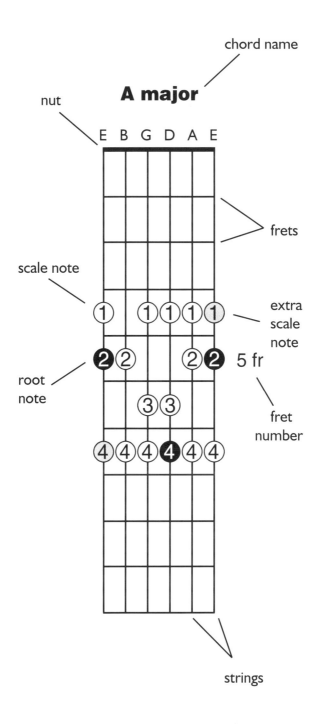

chord name

nut

A major

scale note

root note

frets

extra scale note

5 fr

fret number

strings

5

SCALE TYPES

For each note six types of scale are given: **major**, **mixolydian**, **natural minor**, **pentatonic minor**, **pentatonic major**, and **blues**.

The major scale

This is the basis for most Western music whether popular or 'classical'. It consists of seven notes arranged in a sequence of intervals: tone, tone, semitone, tone, tone, tone, semitone. In frets this would be 2-2-1-2-2-2-1. You can test this for yourself. Hold down any note on any string below the 5th fret. Play it, then move up the string according to the 2-2-1-2-2-2-1 distances, playing each note as you go. You will hear a major scale. But obviously, going up on one string is not a good pattern for the fingers!

The mixolydian

Despite its exotic name, this scale is simply the major scale with the 7th note lowered by a semitone, giving an interval pattern of 2-2-1-2-2-1-2. Since blues, soul, rock and folk often have the lowered seventh in their harmony this is a common sound.

The natural minor

The minor scale most used in popular music is the natural minor. Its pattern of intervals is 2-1-2-2-1-2-2, adding two notes to the pentatonic minor. These notes can be very expressive, bringing a new dimension to the five we were using.

The pentatonic minor

'Pentatonic' means five notes. The interval pattern is 3-2-2-3-2. In its various forms the pentatonic is the most popular scale pattern for lead guitar, and is often the scale which most people first learn on the guitar. It gives a distinct, tough sound, especially in major key blues.

The pentatonic major

The pentatonic also has a major form, interval pattern 2-2-3-2-3. This is simply notes 1, 2, 3, 5 and 6 of the major scale. In comparison to the pentatonic minor the major form has a happy, bright, upbeat character.

The blues scale

By adding one note to the pentatonic minor we get what is known as the 'blues scale'. The extra note is the lowered 5th, giving an interval pattern of 3-2-1-1-3-2. This is used in blues and rock, and lends a darker tone to the pentatonic minor.

Arpeggios

After the six scales you will find two arpeggio boxes. An arpeggio is a musical figure created by taking the three notes of a chord and playing them sequentially through one or more octaves. These are sometimes used in lead solos to contrast with the step-by-step movement of scale-based playing.

OPEN AND MOVEABLE FINGERINGS

In order to demonstrate the variety of first position scale patterns in all the keys open strings have been included. These patterns can only be played in the given place. However some of the scales have no open strings; these patterns are moveable. You can select whichever root note you would like to start the scale on, and repeat the pattern from that note. As long as you keep the pattern the same in the new position you will produce the same type of scale on the new root note.

Master shapes

The key moveable shapes we will term '**master shapes**'. There are 12, two for each type of scale, one with the root on the 5th string and the other starting on the 6th. The six master shapes for scales that start on the 6th are the A scales; for ones that start on the 5th string see the boxes for C♯ / D♭.

If you are a complete beginner try C major, G major, and the E and F scale boxes. These have some of the easiest fingering.

If you play with a pick, use alternating down and up strokes throughout the scales. If you play with your fingers, use alternating index and middle fingers.

SCALES BASED ON A

A major is a popular key for the guitar, and you'll find these patterns very useful. All six are moveable and can therefore be played starting from almost any fret on the sixth string.

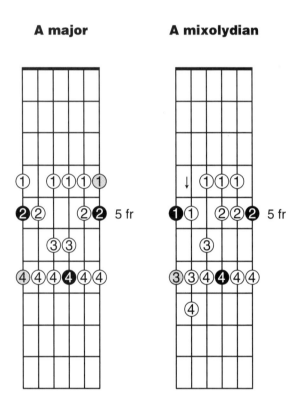

A major   **A mixolydian**

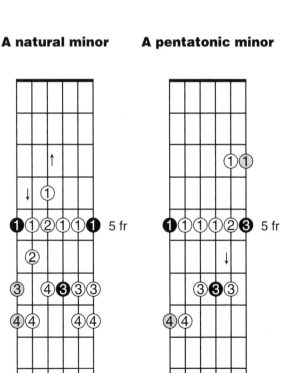

A natural minor   **A pentatonic minor**

Notice how the A major scale stays in a single 'box' of four frets. The first finger is always at the fourth fret here. This is what is known as 'fourth position'. Some scales require a change of position, as with the A mixolydian.

A pentatonic major   **A blues scale**

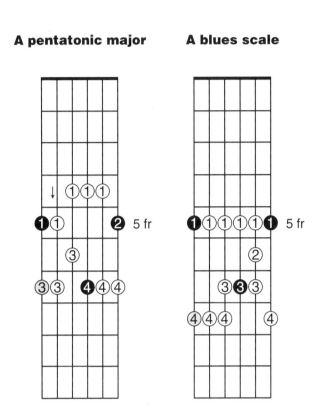

Arpeggio: A major   **Arpeggio: A minor**

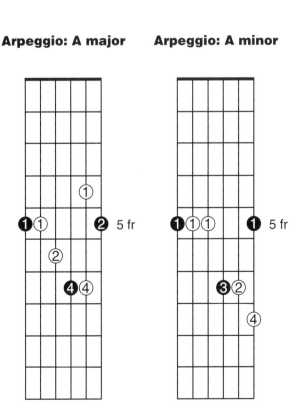

SCALES BASED ON A♯/B♭

Guitar-based music tends not to be found in flat keys, though B♭ major still uses some of the open strings as these scales demonstrate. Notice with B♭ natural minor that there is a shift to 4th

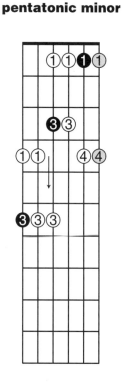

A♯/B♭ major

A♯/B♭ mixolydian

A♯/B♭ natural minor

A♯/B♭ pentatonic minor

position on the 3rd string but the 1st finger isn't actually used at the 4th fret until you get to the 2nd string. Watch out for the 3 fret 'jump' in the B♭ blues scale.

A♯/B♭ pentatonic major   **A♯/B♭ blues scale**

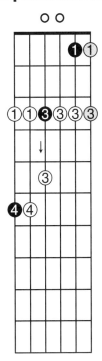
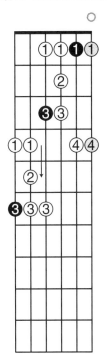

Arpeggio:
A♯/B♭ major

Arpeggio:
A♯/B♭ minor

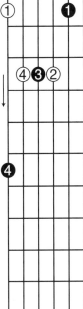
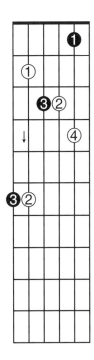

SCALES BASED ON B

The B major, mixolydian and natural minor patterns all take advantage of the open 2nd B string before moving up. Notice that all the open strings can be used in B minor.

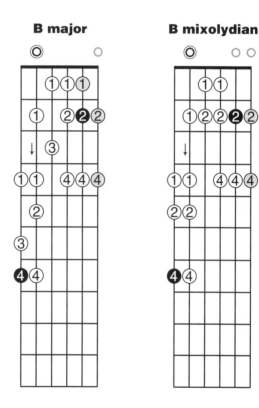

B major

B mixolydian

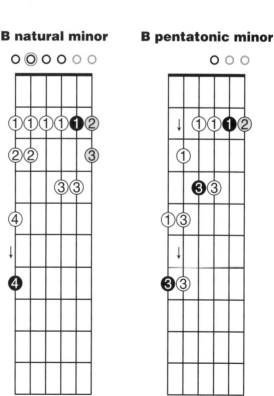

B natural minor

B pentatonic minor

The B pentatonic major is a very important moveable pattern which can start from anywhere on the 5th string.

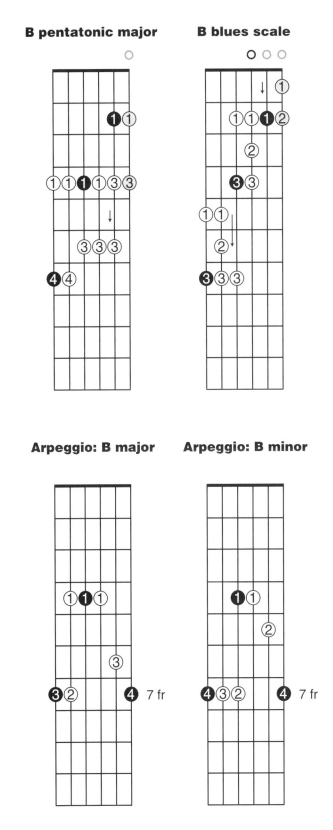

B pentatonic major

B blues scale

Arpeggio: B major

Arpeggio: B minor

7 fr

SCALES BASED ON C

C major is a popular guitar key. The open strings are all 'in key' and many of the chords have resonant open string shapes that are easy to play. The C major scale is an excellent beginner's pattern. If you have never played any scales before this is a good one to start with.

C major

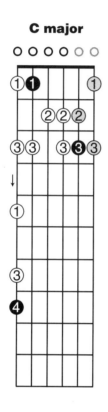

C mixolydian

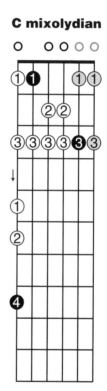

C natural minor

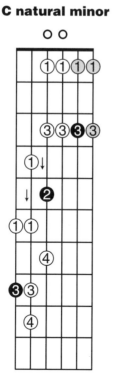

C pentatonic minor

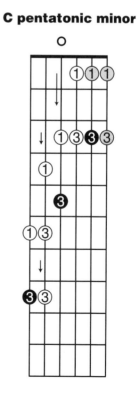

C natural minor is a great scale for using in solo patterns – it's easy to pull off to the open third and fourth strings. The C pentatonic minor is another useful moveable pattern that will give you any pentatonic minor whose root is at the 3rd fret or higher on the 5th string.

C pentatonic major   C blues scale

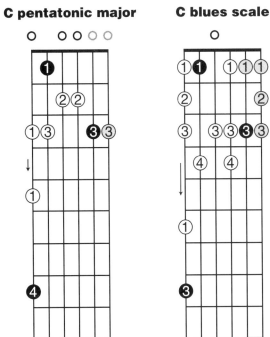

Arpeggio: C major   Arpeggio: C minor

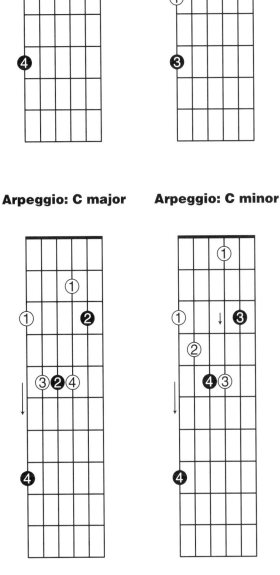

SCALES BASED ON C#/D♭

None of the guitar's open string notes are in the scale of C♯ / D♭ major, although A, B and E occur in C♯ minor (which in D♭ minor would be B♭♭, C♭ and F♭ – same pitch, just different names!).

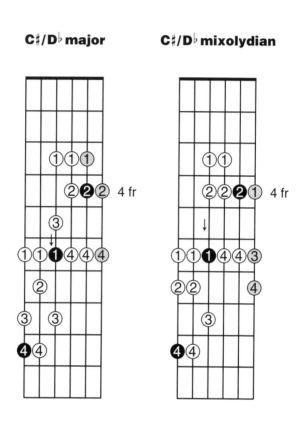

C♯/D♭ major   **C♯/D♭ mixolydian**

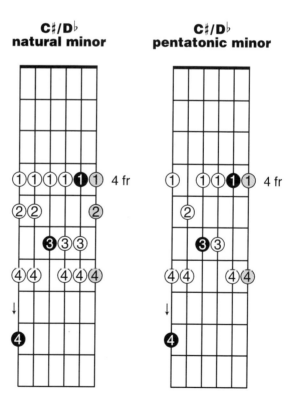

C♯/D♭ natural minor   **C♯/D♭ pentatonic minor**

C♯/D♭ pentatonic major

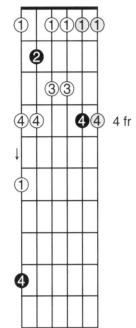

4 fr

C♯/D♭ blues scale

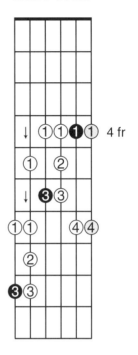

4 fr

Arpeggio: C♯/D♭ major

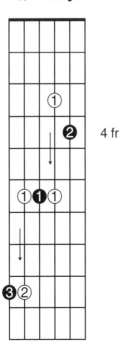

4 fr

Arpeggio: C♯/D♭ minor

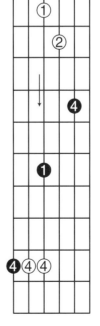

4 fr

SCALES BASED ON D

Like C, D major is another popular guitar key, which uses nice easy chords, and open strings in the scale. Remember to start the scale on the open D string, otherwise it will sound strange!

D major

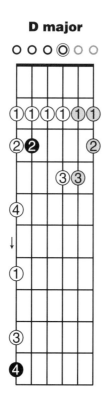

D mixolydian

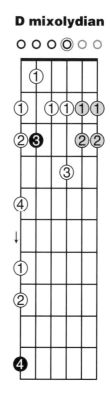

D natural minor

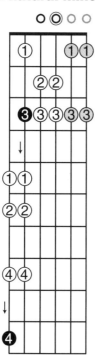

D pentatonic minor

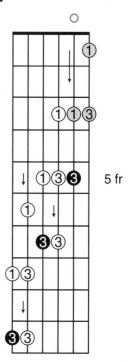

Look out for the two shifts in D natural minor and three in D pentatonic major. The arpeggios are based on two well-known chord shapes that you might be familiar with.

D pentatonic minor

D blues scale

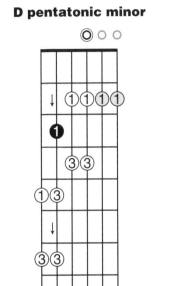

Arpeggio: D major

Arpeggio: D minor

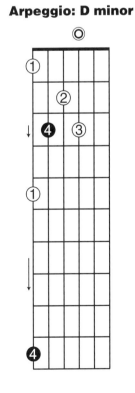

SCALES BASED ON D#/E♭

Like C#/D♭, D#/E♭ is not a popular key for the guitar since it doesn't use the lowest bass note, and many of the chords are barre chords. Guitar songs in the key of E♭ are often played with a capo.

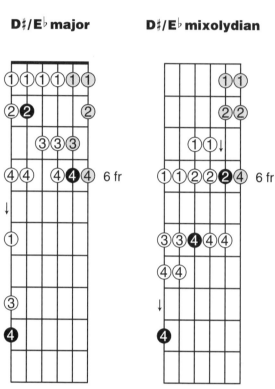

D#/E♭ major   D#/E♭ mixolydian

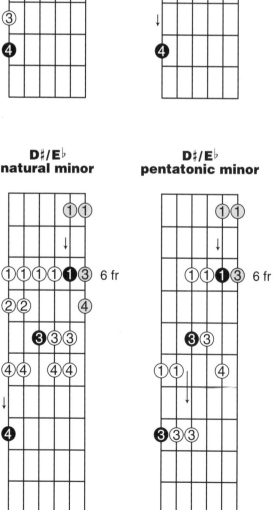

D#/E♭ natural minor   D#/E♭ pentatonic minor

D♯/E♭ pentatonic minor

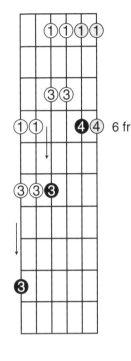

D♯/E♭ blues scale

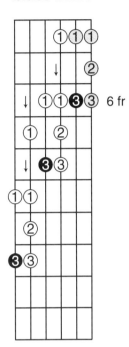

Arpeggio: D♯/E♭ major

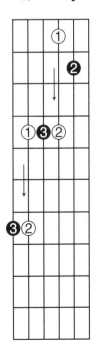

Arpeggio: D♯/E♭ minor

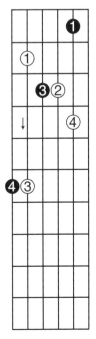

SCALES BASED ON E

If the guitar has a true 'home' key it's E minor (the open strings actually make an Em7add11 chord) closely followed by E major.

E major

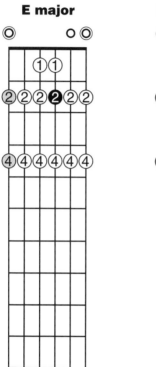

E mixolydian

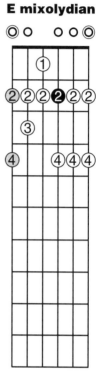

E natural minor

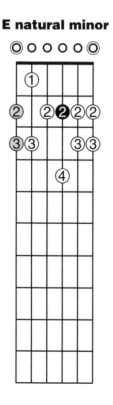

E pentatonic minor

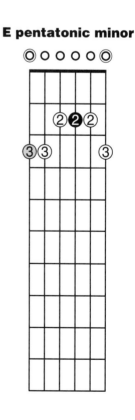

All six scales are in open position to take advantage of the open strings, though of course you could play any of them as a moveable pattern higher up the neck.

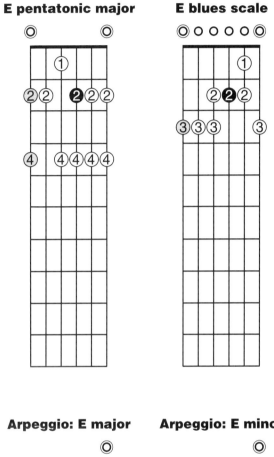

E pentatonic major

E blues scale

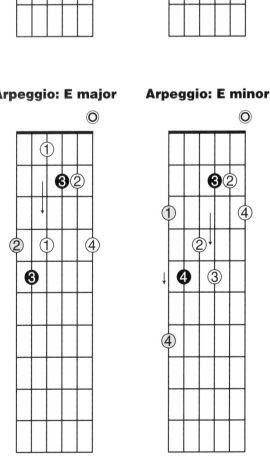

Arpeggio: E major

Arpeggio: E minor

SCALES BASED ON F

With only a single flat note (B♭), F major allows for more open string playing, even if it introduces a number of barre chords. This F major scale is a good beginner's pattern.

F major

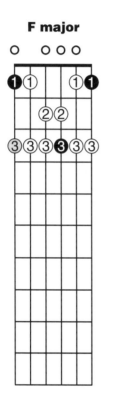

F mixolydian

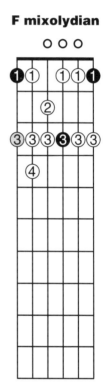

F natural minor

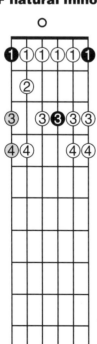

F pentatonic minor

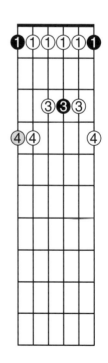

F minor is one of the guitar's least-used minor keys, mainly because it soon gets tiring holding down a full barre F minor at the first fret for any length of time.

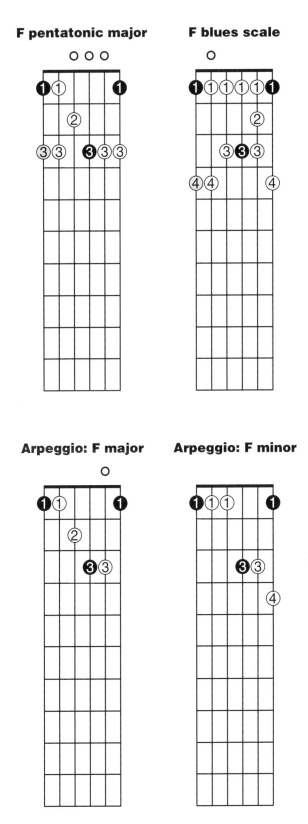

F pentatonic major

F blues scale

Arpeggio: F major

Arpeggio: F minor

SCALES BASED ON F♯/G♭

As an extreme sharp / flat key, F♯/G♭ is not used much by guitarists as all the important chords are barre chords. The first box is a master shape for

F♯/G♭ major   F♯/G♭ mixolydian

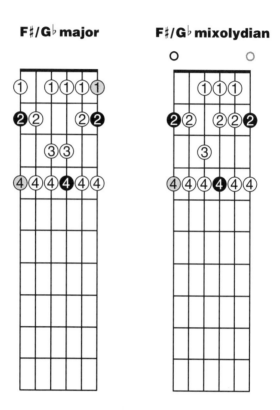

F♯/G♭ natural minor F♯/G♭ pentatonic minor

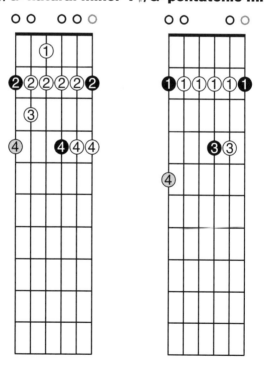

any major scale whose root is on the 6th string, with no position shifts. The second is a master shape for the mixolydian.

F♯/G♭ pentatonic major

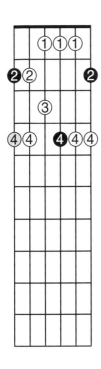

F♯/G♭ blues scale

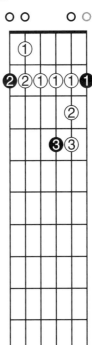

**Arpeggio:
F♯/G♭ major**

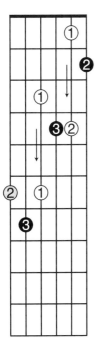

**Arpeggio:
F♯/G♭ minor**

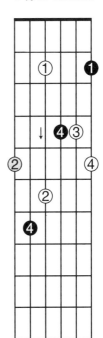

SCALES BASED ON G

Home to several of the guitar's most resonant open string chords, G major sees the return of abundant open strings. These patterns are nice and easy for beginners.

G minor

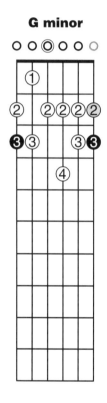

G mixolydian

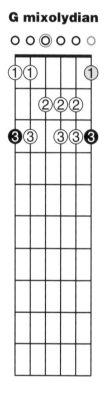

G natural minor

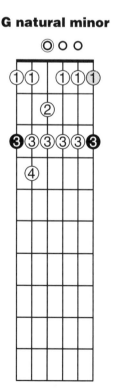

G pentatonic minor

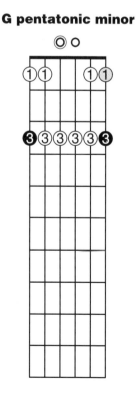

Notice the unusual symmetry of the G pentatonic minor, with the 3rd finger on the 3rd fret on every string, and the fact that you only use two fingers for the pentatonic major!

G pentatonic major

G blues scale

Arpeggio: G major

Arpeggio: G minor

SCALES BASED ON G♯/A♭

We finish with another of those unfriendly keys that uses lots of barre chords. The major box starting on the little finger is another master pattern. The pentatonic major and blues scale boxes will give you a chance to really travel across

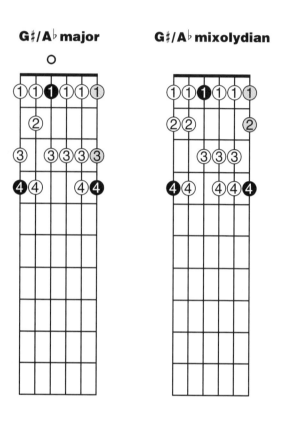

G♯/A♭ major   **G♯/A♭ mixolydian**

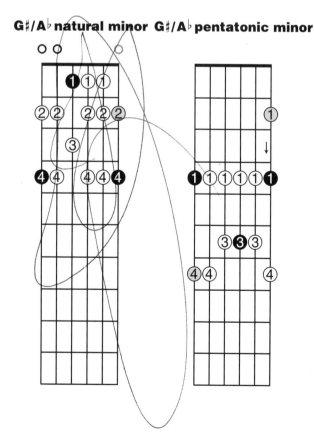

G♯/A♭ natural minor   G♯/A♭ pentatonic minor

the fretboard. This book concentrates on two-octave scales – but you can invent patterns that will give you an extra octave by using carefully planned shifts of position that progress using this kind of movement.

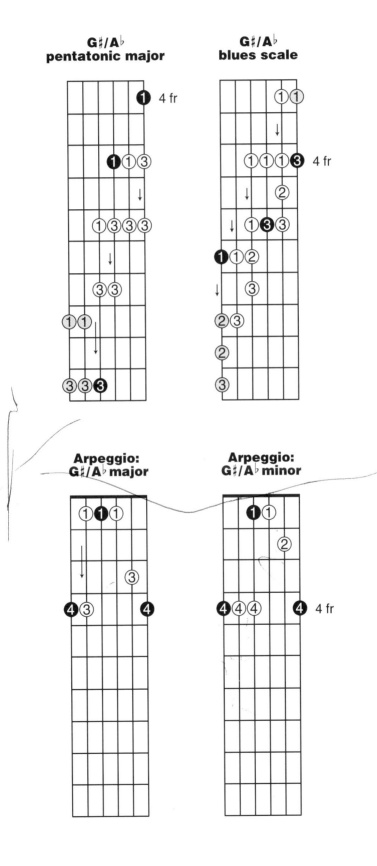

G♯/A♭ pentatonic major

G♯/A♭ blues scale

Arpeggio: G♯/A♭ major

Arpeggio: G♯/A♭ minor

FURTHER READING

If you've enjoyed this book, why not check out some of the other great titles suitable for your guitar case, available from all good music and book shops, or in case of difficulty, directly from Music Sales (see p2) or **www.musicroom.com**.

The Guitar Case Guide To Left-Handed Chords
AM970684
Over 180 of the most useful chords, specially arranged for left-handers, using clear diagrams and handy tips.

The Gig Bag Book Of Arpeggios For All Guitarists
AM946902
The ultimate arpeggio reference book for all guitarists, containing 240 arpeggios in all 12 keys. The handy fretboard diagrams illustrate the finger positions.

The Gig Bag Book Of Guitar TAB Chords
AM943250
Over 2,100 chords for all guitarists, compiled by Mark Bridges and presented in unique guitar TAB format. Each diagram illustrates the fingering, inversion and notes of every chord.

The Original Guitar Case Scale Book
AM76217
In this volume Peter Pickow gives guitarists a concise thesaurus of essential and practical forms for study and practice. Tips on using scales to build speed, endurance and fretboard fluency.

Guitar Case Chord Book
AM35841
The original essential chord book for your guitar case, with over 100 chords grouped by key, in all 12 keys.